Evolving

Pamela Benson

Copyright © 2024 Pamela Benson

All rights reserved.

No part of this book may be reproduced, stored in a retrieval system, or transmitted, in any form or by any means, electronic, mechanical, photocopying, recording, or otherwise, without prior written permission from the publisher, except for brief quotations embodied in critical reviews and certain other noncommercial uses permitted by copyright law.

ISBN: 978-1-963949-61-2

Printed in the United States of America

A Little About the Author

Pamela Benson was born in Seaford, Delaware, on December 17, 1970, at Nanticoke Hospital to Lester and Lola Benson. Her mother's former last name was Jones. Her mother was named Elsie Batts, and she was a pastor in Coverdale, Delaware. Her father was Frankie Wolford, and his employment was unknown. Her father's mother's name was Pearl Benson, and her grandfather's name was George Benson. They lived in Concord, Delaware, on the slave masters' land, where they raised chickens and grew grapes. They were very poor with money but rich in God's spirit. Pamela's family is very large but disconnected. Pamela Benson has 4 children, 3 girls and one boy and 5 grandchildren. Her mother and father are deceased, along with their parents. She has 1 aunt who is alive on her dad's side of the family, and her mother did not have any brothers or sisters. She has 3 sisters and 2 brothers, and a lot of nephews and nieces. Her journey consists of going back to school after receiving her Ged in 2011 and then going into the RN program, which she dropped down due to some family problems. She went to Brightwood Institute in 2015 as a medical assistant. In 2021, during a rough time, she decided to go back to AIU, which is a university for her Bachelor of Healthcare Management, and she will graduate in May 2025. For her bachelor's degree, she will open a small senior citizen home, which will consist of a couple of homeless residents. As of now, she provides services to the community by offering home health services in several states. During the summer, she travels to Florida with her long-time client. She and her daughter have been members of Elevated Life in Christ Community Church for 7 years. She services her senior community by helping with in-home care or cleaning for the ones who can not clean themselves. She is also in a class called Journey through the heart of God, which is run by her own pastor.

Acknowledgments

I wanted to applaud my Best friend, Ronnier Henry, we went to elementary school together and we reconnected a couple of years ago not knowing he was going to be one of my biggest cheerleaders my pusher, along with some other people but he would always say Pam you should write a book and I would say when God directs me. I never thought my life was worthy to be told but as I think about it, it really is. I have suffered in silence for so long, as a young girl I lived a life of trauma being thrown into chaos and drama by my parents, to me it is very selfish to bring children into the world of the unknown, they are not knowing or understanding their life so they just put you in their mess. Ronnier is a very educated African American man who studies law and gives excellent advice. We can be on the phone talking about anything, from God to law and slavery. I thank him for giving me a push. I know at times I get stubborn and it takes a little to catch what other people see. I would also like to thank my Pastor Veronica Dixon. Without her, I never felt like I was able to have the courage to do any of this. I now understand how to be confident and have high self-esteem. I stand and do not care what others say or how they look, because this is my story and not theirs!

Thank God for connections 🙏

Table of content

Chapter 1 – Evaporation 1

Chapter 2 – The House That Divided 5

Chapter 3 – Time to Birth 10

Chapter 4 – New Beginnings with new love 29

Chapter 5 – What does love have to do with it! 33

Chapter 6 – Escaping a Narcissist and being able to
tell the story! 49

Chapter 1

Evaporation

I believe that, even at an early age, I was protected by God. Chaos seemed to surround me, and I often didn't know what to do. I prayed, and while it seemed like my prayers were not being heard, they actually were, because I was able to endure situations that would have caused others to faint or even consider suicide. Born into a world designed for adults, my God sustained me.

Deuteronomy 32:36

The Lord will rescue his people when he sees that their strength is gone. He will have mercy on those who serve him when he sees how helpless they are.

Evaporation

In life, you make plans, hoping they will go accordingly. As a young mother, when you have children, you want the best for them. But sometimes, life doesn't go the way you planned. Sometimes, it leaves you with deep wounds and scars, and you start reliving the thoughts of the life you once envisioned for yourself. You become angry, and then sadness takes over. Over the years, that sadness can turn into depression.

Well, this story will blow your mind, and may leave you feeling both sad and mad. It's about the life of a young girl whose fate was placed in the hands of someone else's trauma. She was unable to live as a child should. Instead, she was forced to give up her youth, adopt an adult mindset, and adjust to the atmosphere of a grown person's world. The child began to act out of feelings, emotions, and helplessness. So, prepare yourself for a journey that will stir your emotions.

In my earlier years, around the ages of six and seven, I was always an inquisitive child, constantly asking questions. I had a heart that felt compelled to care for anything. During my days after school or on weekends, when I had nothing else to do, I would find animals to tend to, puppies, kittens, turtles, ants, butterflies, anything I could nurture. This was the beginning of my ministry, though I didn't know it at the time. I loved the feeling it gave me, and looking back, it was the start of my calling.

I was always a quiet child, content with being by myself and never getting into too much trouble. I was very obedient, always doing everything I could to make my parents happy. I loved to learn and always wore a smile on my face. Life, to me at that time, was great. I was a little tomboy, not really understanding too much about the world. Whenever I asked questions, my mother would tell me I talked too much or asked too many questions. If I asked for something, I was often told I begged too much. I thought that because she was my mom, this was just the way things were supposed to be.

I believed everything was fine, until my heart was broken over and over again by my own mother. All I wanted was time and love from my parents. I couldn't understand why I was treated as though I had done something wrong. All I wanted was answers to the questions I asked. What had I done to deserve this? What did I do?

This is why I often shut down. I would go climb trees or head out to the field to do cartwheels by myself. I would collect things that needed my attention. I didn't have many friends, and the ones I did have, I didn't really understand. I was always just that little girl, wandering and slowly realizing that life was hard and sad.

When I was in the 4th grade, more problems began to arise. I was never bullied, but my attention span was short. I think the school tried to reach out to my mom, but because of her own issues, she never attended the meetings. I remember her coming once. I'm pretty sure she cursed the staff out; maybe she was even banned, I don't know. Eventually, they put me in speech therapy.

I believe that if my mother had not silenced me or criticized me for speaking, I might have been able to improve my speech. I remember them sending papers home for her to sign, and she would sign everything without asking questions. One of those papers allowed them to place me in special education. It wasn't because I was slow or unable to learn, I stopped trying to do my work because I felt sad most of the time. Instead of someone asking, "How can I help you?" they just pushed me out of the way.

I didn't understand why this was happening. I understood the schoolwork, but I was different, I was just trying to make sense of why I felt the way I did. Why was I like this? Why wouldn't anyone help me?

At that time, no one in my family expressed love verbally, but I found ways to show it. Every Mother's Day or birthday, if I could buy my mom something, I would. I felt sad for her most of the time, and sometimes I was angry, but I could never stay that way. I prayed all the time, often inside our coat closet, which became my secret place.

I think my grandmother may have taught me how to pray. She was the only one who seemed to care about my well-being. I loved her dearly. Some nights, we would stay at her house, which was on land left to her family by a former slave master. They had grapevines and chickens, and she would cook. It felt like an unjudged place, filled with love. But they had an outhouse, and I was always scared to go out there.

This was my dad's mom, and being at her house felt like a temporary escape. I was just a little girl, left to figure out the what, the where, and the how of my life.

I'll never know exactly what my family went through, but I see families today who have survived similar struggles. Somewhere along the line, though, my family became disconnected. When you bring children into an already chaotic world and into a family that is simply trying to survive, I believe you're setting the stage for more trouble. At that point, it's selfishness.

Lord Teach Me Your Ways!

Chapter 2

The House That Divided

My life took a turn for the worse at the age of nine when my dad decided to leave. I remember it as clearly as if it were yesterday. That day felt different. My mom had been on the phone with my dad, and she was crying. Later that night, my dad came in through the back door and told me not to tell my mom he was there. I didn't say anything. He began packing his clothes, and I asked him where he was going. He said he would be back, but I don't remember him coming back for a very long time.

I didn't understand what was happening, and I didn't ask a lot of questions. All I knew was that our house suddenly felt empty. My mom was pregnant, and I later found out the baby wasn't my dad's. After a while, things seemed quiet, but then my mom started partying and drinking heavily. Her behavior changed, she became verbally abusive toward me and physically abusive to my brothers and sister.

Some days, I went to school in dirty clothes with no breakfast. Sometimes, I had to comb my hair with a fork because there was no other option. I started acting out in school, full of anger and frustration. I was furious that my mom would stay in bed for days, drunk, while everything around us fell apart.

My mom did have a boyfriend during this time, and I liked him. He took care of us, he was kind, and I think he genuinely loved my mom. But one day, my mom threw hot grease on him. He was about to hit her, and I jumped in the middle to stop him. I became the mediator between them, which I shouldn't have had to do as a child. I just happened to stay home from school that day, which is how I ended up witnessing the whole thing.

Despite everything, I loved my mom. And in her own way, I knew she loved me too. But even with that love, I was going through things no child should have to endure, so much stress and so many tears.

When I was 13 years old, I met a friend and started spending time at her house to escape the drama and chaos at home. During this time, my friend had a boyfriend who was older than her. One night, I was scared to walk home, so he offered to walk me. However, during the walk, he made sexual advances toward me. At that point in my life, I had never had sex before. The most he did was perform a little oral sex on me, but I stopped him because it didn't feel right, he was my friend's boyfriend, after all. I eventually got home that night.

For months, he kept pursuing me. Every time he saw me, it was the same thing. Then, one particular night, my mom was really getting on my nerves. I didn't understand why she acted the way she did, and I just wanted to get away from the chaos at home. That's when I decided to stay with Tom, who had a thing for younger women. I thought staying with him would give me a break from my mom's house for a while. After a few months of being involved with Tom, I stopped seeing him.

Not long after, Tom's brother asked me to go out with him. I agreed, and this became another way to escape my house. I was involved with him for a few months, but eventually, I stopped seeing him as well. Both Tom and his brother served the same purpose, they were an escape from my mom's toxic environment.

Meanwhile, my friend (Tom's girlfriend) became pregnant. By that time, I had no interest in Tom anymore. I was introduced to another guy who seemed cool, and we ended up having sex. After a while, I found out I was pregnant. This baby wasn't Tom's; it was someone else's. He was 2 ½ years older than me. I was 14 ½ years old and terrified of what my mom would do when she found out.

What made it worse was that I had gone to my mom months earlier to ask about getting on birth control, but she ignored my request. By the time I realized I was pregnant, I was already four months along.

One night, my mom brought a man home and introduced him to me. When he shook my hand, he ran his fingers through my palm. I knew what that meant, it was a sexual gesture. I told my mom what had happened, but she didn't take me seriously. Her reaction hurt me deeply. I was disturbed by the entire situation.

That night, no one in the house slept. I stayed up all night, angry and heartbroken. I couldn't believe my mom would choose a man she barely knew over me, but deep down, I guess I wasn't surprised.

I didn't know what to do or how to process everything. All I knew was that I was pregnant, with a human growing inside my body. I hadn't even had a proper conversation with anyone about sex, my body, or pregnancy. I had no idea what to expect.

At five months pregnant, I started attending DAPI, a school for pregnant teen mothers. It was a blessing. They taught us about our bodies and what to expect during pregnancy. We also took general education classes, which was amazing. I met other girls who were going through the same thing as me, and it helped me feel less alone.

As my baby grew, my mom's behavior got worse. I knew I didn't want my child to grow up in the same environment I did. One day, as my due date approached, I stopped in the living room and prayed. I gave my baby back to God, trusting that He would protect her no matter what happened.

I was just a scared young woman who hadn't even lived her life yet. I was in the 8th grade when I got pregnant, with no knowledge of life or my body. I was excited about my baby, but I was terrified too, terrified that she would have to come into this world and suffer as I had.

When it was time to deliver, I felt both excited and scared. I didn't know what to expect. I was in labor for a whole day, but I wasn't in any pain. Later, I found out I have what's called a tilted uterus. Doctors say it's a miracle I was able to get pregnant at all. On top of that, my pelvic bones don't open like they normally should, so I was scheduled for a C-section.

I was scared because I didn't know what to expect during the surgery. I prayed before going to the hospital. My baby had been trying to escape the womb, but due to my condition, she couldn't. She had to wait.

When I got to the hospital, I lay there for 12 hours before the doctors finally decided to prepare me for my C-section. A while later, my baby was delivered safely.

I remember the time when it was finally time for me to have my baby. I was scared and emotional, unsure of what was going to happen. Being so young, my thoughts swirled around in my mind endlessly. "What am I going to do?" That question kept repeating in my head, especially as I tried to find a job and was turned down over and over again.

This life, the one I found myself living, was not the life I wanted. But I now realize that the struggles I went through shaped me into the person I am today. I have always been strong and independent, but the noise and chaos in my life forced me to make up my mind about who I wanted to become. The struggles of hunger and cold made me determined not to remain stuck in that place.

Hard times teach you to work harder, to break free from the stagnant mindset of "this is all I can be." In reality, life's challenges push you to give birth to your dreams and make them a reality. For me, my daughter was the push I needed. She became my reason to fight harder and the inspiration I needed to turn my dreams into reality.

Psalms 127:3-4

No doubt about it: children are a gift from the Lord, the fruit of the womb is a divine reward. The children born when is young are like the arrows in the hand of a warrior

Chapter 3

Time to Birth

Well, it was time to give birth. I was at Milford Hospital, and my mom was with me. She was such a beautiful woman when she wasn't drinking. On June 28, 1986, I gave birth to the most beautiful baby I had ever seen. She weighed 8.7 pounds and was 21 inches long, with a head full of hair. But I was scared, not for me, but for her. She was coming into this crazy world, and I didn't want her to be tainted by anything.

I wanted to keep her safe and give her everything she needed, but I was only 15, not even old enough to get a real job. Yet, God provided for us through people. She had diapers, clothes, a bassinet, and formula. Everything we needed was somehow given to us until I was able to find a way to provide for her on my own.

I was determined to take care of my baby. She was mine, and I loved her deeply. I eventually got a job, but I assumed my mom would help with transportation. She wouldn't. So, every morning, I packed up my things and got my baby ready. I walked her to a lady's house in Georgetown, Delaware, someone I knew who agreed to watch her while I worked. From there, I would walk to work, which took about an hour. It was hard, but I was willing to do anything for my daughter.

I kept at it for a while until the job ended and they didn't need me anymore. After that, I wanted to go back to school. You know, in my community, getting pregnant and quitting school was the norm, but to me, it felt backward. I wanted to be better.

We stayed at my mom's house, but there was always so much drama with her. I remember one morning, I was making breakfast for my baby when my mom suddenly said, "I'm going to call the cops on you." I was shocked and asked her, "For what?" At that point, I was so sick and tired of always trying to do right by her, only for nothing I did to ever be good enough.

Luckily, my sister happened to be visiting from North Carolina around that time, so I asked her if I could go back with her. She and her husband agreed, and we left. But after staying with them for a while, I discovered her husband was abusive toward her. To protect us, she sent me and my baby to live with my dad.

I was 17 by then, and I was so tired of all the mess and drama. I didn't know whether my dad wanted us there or not, but we had nowhere else to go. I never understood why my parents treated me like I was some kind of plague. I never asked to be born. If they didn't want me, they could have just given me up for adoption. I was tired, but I had to protect my baby.

We moved in with my dad, his wife, and my stepsister. I went back to school and worked hard to catch up. That summer, I was able to test out of the 11th grade and go straight into the 12th. But my stepmom was so evil. All I wanted was to graduate and leave.

Eventually, after a year of being treated like I didn't matter and being blamed for things I wasn't even involved in, I left. I had to find a place for me and my baby, far away from that house. I prayed constantly, asking God, Why me? Why is my life like this? I'm so tired.

I tried to reconnect with my mom so I could at least graduate high school, but that didn't work out either. We ended up bouncing from house to house. My heart was breaking, but I couldn't give up, not for me and not for my baby.

One day, I found myself walking through a town called Concord. A man noticed me, and that man would eventually become my son's father. After meeting him and his mom, she started asking me questions about my situation. I told her the truth: I had nowhere to live, and I had a baby to take care of. To my surprise, she let us stay with them.

I remember feeling such relief. I said to myself, Yes, finally. My daughter was two years old by then. I signed her up for Head Start, and for the first time in a long time, I started to feel a sense of normalcy. I could finally see greater things ahead for my little girl.

I was determined that my daughter was going to learn everything I didn't, and I was going to show her love, the kind of love I was never shown or told about. But I understood that people could only give you what they knew how to give.

One day, I was talking to my daughter's father on the phone while my boyfriend was in the room. He became jealous, and after I hung up the phone, he hit me. It was the first time I had ever been hit. He started talking as if he had accomplished something, like hitting me made him powerful. That day, I went into the kitchen, grabbed a knife, and stabbed him. No man was going to hit me, I wouldn't allow it. My parents may not have loved me the way I needed, but they never hit me.

At age 18, we were still living at my boyfriend's mother's house. My daughter's father would come to get her every other weekend, faithfully, and I was happy about that. But one particular night, my mind went to a dark place. I started thinking that my baby might be better off without me. I went into the bathroom, took some pills, and laid on the bed, thinking I would just fall asleep. But God had other plans.

He didn't let me close my eyes. Instead, He ministered to me, asking, "Who is going to love your daughter better than you?" I began to cry as He kept reminding me, "Your baby needs you." All

I could do was lie there, staring at the ceiling with tears in my eyes. My life wasn't going well, but my baby's life was. She loved her mother, and I loved her. God healed me that night, and the next morning, I woke up grateful to be alive and to see my daughter when she came back.

I decided to start putting in applications for apartments. A while later, I found out I was pregnant again, and soon after that, I got a place. I didn't really want my boyfriend to move in with us, but he ended up coming too. He was abusive, even during my pregnancy.

He was on drugs, and one day at the apartment, we got into a fight. He asked me for money, and I told him no. I can't even recall how it escalated, but at some point, he put his hands on me. I remember throwing alcohol on him in the bathroom, and he slipped. As he got up, he hit me on the side of my lip and locked the bathroom door because I was ready to stab him. I don't even know why I stayed in that mess of a relationship. When I told his mother what was happening, she manipulated me into keeping him there. It was exhausting.

I gave birth to my son on November 13, 1990, and I was determined to do better. But the truth is, if no one shows you how to have better, it's hard to know how to achieve it. That Christmas, he didn't even come home. Instead, he sent a bag of diapers with a young man who lived in the complex.

I couldn't let him ruin my children's Christmas, so I took action. I got someone to watch my kids, his oldest son's aunt, and I walked into town to find him. Drugs don't care about anyone, but I wasn't going to let them control my children's happiness. I searched high and low, and when I finally found him, I got my money. I told him he wouldn't be coming back until he gave me what I needed for my children.

I don't know why I felt so obligated to keep this grown man around, but I was tired of his mess. Thankfully, my best friend lived next door, and that was a blessing. She would watch my children, and I would watch hers. Both of us came from broken homes, and we were just trying to find ourselves in the midst of our struggles.

In 1992, I lost my apartment and moved to Concord Trailer Park. I got a job at Allen's Chicken Factory. They had a bus that came to pick you up for work, and my boyfriend's aunt would watch the children. For a while, things worked out. But then the bus service stopped, and I ended up relying on welfare, something I did not like.

It seemed like a struggle everywhere I turned, no matter how hard I tried. I told myself, Something has to change. I don't know how, but something has to happen.

I decided to get rid of my son's father, and we moved into a house apartment. But I was pregnant again. This time, I got involved with my son's father's cousin. He was just as messed up as the first situation. Honestly, he was just a replacement at that time. It was never supposed to turn into anything serious, but here we go again.

I had everything set up for my kids: daycare was arranged, I was working at another Hardee's, and I was also trying to get my GED because I knew there had to be something better out there in the world. But sometimes, when you get into these situations, it's hard to get out of them.

On August 17, 1993, I gave birth to a little girl. She was 6 pounds, 2 ounces, and 20 inches long, cute as a button. Her dad was in jail, which I was honestly fine with because that meant I didn't have to deal with him.

In September 1994, her dad called me from the halfway house he was staying in. He asked me to bring him some clothes. I said I would, but I needed to find someone to watch my children. There weren't many people I trusted to care for them, but I ended up asking his mother, and she agreed.

That Saturday, my cousin and best friend took me to drop off my kids at his mother's house. My baby was wearing a yellow snowsuit that day. I remember this because my little girl cried a lot, and her grandmother knew that. That's one of the reasons I didn't leave my children with many people.

After dropping them off, I tried to find the halfway house but couldn't. Frustrated, I called my dad and stepmom to come pick me up. My stepmom wanted me to stay at their place, but something in my spirit told me to leave, so I did. When I got to the Delaware bus station, I called my cousin, and they came to get me. We went to my cousin's house, and I picked up my children on the way.

Here's where things started to go wrong. When I picked up my baby, she was still in the same yellow snowsuit I had left her in, and she was hollering and sweating. I picked her up, and she stopped crying. But when we got to my cousin's house, I took her snowsuit off and noticed a fresh scratch on her neck. I immediately called her grandmother to ask about it, but she lied. After that, I never let her watch my children again.

Now, this next part is hard to talk about, but it's part of my story.

One day, we were at the laundromat, and my oldest daughter accidentally dropped my baby. I checked her over, and she seemed fine at the time. A week or two later, my best friend's mom watched my children and brought them back early the next morning. When she returned them, my baby didn't look right. I took off her snowsuit and realized she wasn't responsive or moving at all.

My first reaction was to walk her to the hospital. I woke my friend up, and her boyfriend started CPR on my baby while someone called an ambulance.

When we got to the hospital, they performed a spinal tap and told me my baby was bleeding from the brain. They did X-rays and discovered she had two fractures. One was recent, from when my oldest daughter had dropped her, and the other was from three months prior. They asked me about it, and at first, I couldn't remember what had happened. But then I realized it must have been from when she was at her grandmother's house.

It was a complete mess. My baby was helicoptered to Christiana Hospital, and she wasn't alert for a while. Caseworkers started coming to my house, and they arranged to take me to the hospital to see her. Every day, I would visit her, talk to her, pray over her, and bathe her.

Eventually, the doctors told me she was going to be released. I was so happy, until I found out she wasn't coming home with me. Instead, she was being placed with a foster family.

She was only six months old. I was crushed. I thought to myself, These people don't know me. I love my children. I don't even spank them. I had to deal with the situation as best as I could. They came to the house to talk about my children and their placement. I was so hurt.

In the meantime, my oldest daughter went to stay with her dad for three months, and my son went to stay with his grandmother. I was a praying mother, and my babies were all I knew. Court proceedings were scheduled, and they began investigating me as a mother. I knew everything would work out because I had nothing to hide.

When the court date arrived, my best friend, her mom, and someone else came with me. We sat outside the courtroom for a long time before I finally got up and asked what was going on. To my surprise, the lady at the desk said, "No one informed you? They had to drop the charges."

I could have done flips. It was over! My children could finally come back home, except for my baby. I had to complete home visits before she could be allowed back. I was living in Seaford, Delaware, at the time. It was a mess, but I knew God would fix everything.

Eventually, we moved to Rehoboth Beach, and my boyfriend moved in with us. He was a family man with two sons and a daughter. I took care of his daughter like she was my own. Every other weekend, we would pick up his boys.

One Sunday, after we dropped them back off, I had a bad feeling. As my boyfriend walked toward the car, a group of guys surrounded him and began beating and kicking him. I ran out, screaming, "Stop! Get off him!" The group scattered, and I helped him into the car before we left.

A few days later, he went to visit his dad, who gave him a gun. That was a bad idea.

A couple of weeks after that, we were getting ready for him to go to work. He took the gun out of the closet. I asked him, "Why are you taking the gun out when you're just getting ready for work?" I don't remember what he said, but the next thing I knew, my hand moved down to my groin, and my leg went cold. There was blood.

I can't even explain that feeling, but the Holy Spirit saved my life that day. I remember laying on the bed and hearing him scream. I told him, "Call 911." Right then, I saw my children, and I told them to go into their bedroom.

I spent three days in the hospital while they monitored me to make sure the bullet didn't travel. When I was discharged, I found out I had lost my place. I packed up my things and moved to North Carolina with my children.

Once there, I found a job, and my sister let me stay in her old trailer. Things were okay for a while, but I needed more. I enrolled at Carteret Community College to earn my Child Education Certificate. I knew there was more out there, and I was determined to find it.

As a mother, my drive was always to make sure my children had the best, but I was also trying to figure out life, which I barely understood. Everywhere I looked, I didn't see any positive role models. I constantly wondered, What am I supposed to do?

My oldest sister and I weren't on the same page. She was angry, and her way of communicating was to curse you out as if that would help. In reality, it pushed me further away. I tried to avoid that negativity as much as possible.

I've always been an inquisitive person. I need answers and explanations. But whenever someone spoke to me harshly, I would shut down and not want to talk at all. I've grown up as a loner, and if being alone is where my peace lies, that's where I'd rather stay.

I prayed often, mostly for my children. My heart was full of love for them. Despite everything we had been through, they were happy kids. They didn't have everything I thought they should, but they didn't care. They were just happy to have me.

As parents, we overthink and stress about what to give our children. But often, all they need is love and presence.

That same year, my sister and I started going out to a club in Harlow, NC.

One particular night, my sister and I got into a fight, all because I was seeing someone she thought I shouldn't be seeing. She knew his child's mother and didn't approve of the relationship. Frustrated, I reacted out of emotion and left the next day, not thinking through the consequences. I went back to Delaware, where I had nothing. My pride led me into more trouble than I could handle.

At the time, I had a baby who was on medication, but I couldn't afford to get her medicine. I thought about reaching out to the foster parent my baby had stayed with less than two years ago. Thinking she might be able to help, I made contact with her, but to my surprise, the lady ended up calling my old caseworker. As a result, my baby was placed back into foster care.

I was heartbroken, but in a strange way, I was relieved. At least she was in a safe home. My life, however, was so backward, and I knew I had made many mistakes.

Eventually, I started to get myself together. After some time, I began working in a chicken plant. My God, I hated it. It was cold, wet, and nasty, and I knew I couldn't do this forever. Something had to change. I was exhausted, not just physically, but mentally. I couldn't stop thinking about my children's future, or even my own.

During this time, I met Jake. I just needed some help, and because he showed interest in me, we got together. I was living in Bridgeville, Delaware, when my best friend told me about a program she was attending. She thought it might help me too. I decided to check it out and told my baby sister to come along, but she didn't. I dropped off my oldest daughter and my son at my mom's house and went to fill out the paperwork.

After answering all the questions, I was accepted into the program, and I was able to start in September 1997. I felt so relieved. Of course, the devil tried to throw obstacles in my way, but God is greater!

In the beginning, I had to catch the bus to Delaware Tech College, where the program was held. But then my aunt, who was taking the same course, started attending as well. That was such a blessing because I faced many challenges, but I stayed focused on earning my CNA certificate.

The best part of the program was that after 16 hours of class time, we were allowed to work at the nursing home in Georgetown, Delaware. I was doing what I loved! My God, I was so excited, I didn't have to work in those awful chicken plants anymore or rely on welfare. Life was finally looking up.

I graduated in November 1997 and kept that same job for a while. But due to transportation issues, I ended up losing it. Instead of applying elsewhere, I decided to return to North Carolina, where my sister let me stay until I got back on my feet.

However, things weren't easy. I had to wait 30 days for my CNA license to transfer from Delaware to North Carolina. On top of that, my oldest sister had her own issues with her life so with that, she would take unexcused behavior towards others which I thought was an issue. I saw a lot of things wrong, and I couldn't wait to move out.

To make matters worse, my husband, Jake, was also an alcoholic and a drug addict. The drama seemed never-ending.

Eventually, we moved into a trailer near my sister's place. Ironically, it was the same trailer I had left years earlier. It was in a small town called Harlow. Harlow was tucked behind Havelock, which was the main town where Cherry Point Marine Corps Air Station was located. Havelock had nice buildings, but Harlow felt like a forgotten place, a town where they put underprivileged people and called it a community.

We lived there for a few years, but I grew tired of feeling like we were just existing. I wanted more for my family and myself. At this point in my life, my baby girl hadn't been born yet.

My sister had come to stay with us while she was pregnant. Her boyfriend even came down to North Carolina to be with her, but a lot of things went wrong, and she ended up going back to Delaware. It was such a mess. It felt like my life was spiraling downward, and I couldn't seem to find a way out.

I was exhausted, trying to be everything to everybody while needing direction myself. But, as always, I kept a smile on my face and kept moving forward.

A few years later, we moved to another part of North Carolina, into a nicer trailer. I got a job at Britthaven Nursing Home. The good thing about working there was that after a while, I was able to get as many hours as I needed. I could even sleep there if I wanted to.

In 1999, I finally had the bullet removed from my thigh. Thankfully, the bullet had traveled downward rather than upward. Thank God!

In 2001, I found out I was pregnant again. I was overjoyed. Even after being shot in my groin years earlier, I was still able to conceive. Where the enemy had tried to discount my baby girl, Shantelle, he failed. God had a perfect plan for both of us.

Shantelle was born on December 12, 2001. She was like an angel, the change I desperately needed in my life. I told God that I would be the best mother I could possibly be, and He helped me do just that. I had prayed for a girl, and God had said yes. He didn't tell me when or how, but He answered my prayer.

Even with Shantelle bringing so much joy, I was still going through many struggles. I was tired of dealing with Jake. His sister had moved in with us, and, as always, I wanted to help her. She signed up for CNA school, and after graduating, she got her own apartment. I was so happy for her.

In June 2001, I started having strange feelings in my stomach, a gut feeling that something wasn't right. It's called discernment, and it was especially strong on this one particular day. That day, I had to go to court, but my gut was nagging at me, so I called home to check on things.

When I called, my line was busy, which was strange because I had two-way calling. I tried again, and my niece answered the phone, crying hysterically. She kept saying, "He's dead! He's dead! They killed him!" I tried to calm her down because I couldn't understand what she was saying.

Finally, she told me her brother was dead. For two weeks leading up to this, I had been having bad feelings in my stomach and had even dreamed about this event. In the dream, I couldn't see a face, but I knew something was going to happen.

At the same time, I was dealing with a lot of issues with Jake. I had made the mistake of allowing his niece to move in with us, and she started dating an older man. Somehow, she got involved with a woman who was on drugs. They became friends, and before long, Jake's niece started smoking crack.

I've always been a hard worker, and my best friend came to visit me during this time. She noticed some suspicious activity involving Jake and his niece. They were basically smoking crack down the road from where we lived.

When I went down there, they ran. That was the last straw for me. I put Jake's niece out of the house. After that, I allowed his sister to move in instead.

During this time, Jake didn't have a driver's license. One day, he was caught driving near our house and ended up going to jail. I was seven months pregnant at the time and completely drained from everything I was going through with this man.

After he got out of jail and Shantelle was a little older, I made up my mind to leave. I wanted to move back to Delaware, so we packed up and moved into a hotel in town while preparing to leave. Looking back, it didn't make much sense, but at the time, I was desperate to get out of Adams Creek. Moving anywhere else felt like a good idea.

I was still working at Britthaven, and I rarely let Jake watch my baby. Usually, my oldest daughter watched her when she was home. On one particular day, though, I got a phone call from the police while I was at work. They told me to come and get my baby because Jake had taken her to a parade. They weren't on the roadway, they were on the strip, but Jake had fallen asleep, and my baby, Shantelle, was crawling down the walkway. Someone noticed her and called the authorities.

I left work immediately, picked up my baby, and told the police to please get him away from me. I was so upset. I took Shantelle back to my daughter to care for her because I knew it wasn't her fault, Jake was a grown man with bad habits.

Eventually, Jake got out of jail for that incident. But, as I've mentioned, he was on drugs. He worked when he could, usually in roofing, but his work wasn't consistent. Around this time, a woman moved into the room next to us. She seemed desperate for a man, anyone's man. I introduced myself, and we became friends, or so I thought.

Soon after, I noticed Jake spending more and more time in her room. One day, about two months after she moved in, I went to her room and found him there. I told both of them, "If you want each other, you can have each other. But don't play with me." They were warned.

I couldn't believe Jake. He was on drugs, an alcoholic, barely worked, and yet he had the audacity to play me like this.

About a week after my conversation with them, I came home from work on my lunch break because Jake called me, saying someone was trying to jump him. When I got home, he wasn't there. I asked my daughter if she had seen him, and she said, "You know where he is, Mom."

I went to the woman's room, but neither of them was there. I didn't have much time since I was on my break, but I thought of another place they might be. Sure enough, when I went to his sister's house, I saw her car outside. I didn't bother knocking at first, I looked through the door, and there he was, lying on her lap.

I knocked and knocked until his sister finally came to the door. The first thing she said was, "I told him." That was all it took. I grabbed Sue (the woman) and beat her. I beat her so bad that I thought I had broken her nose. I was ready to go after Jake too, but instead, I told them, "Don't play with me. This is your result." Then I left.

I was shaken up afterward because I thought I had seriously hurt her. I went back to work, worried she might call the cops, but then I realized she was on probation and probably wouldn't report anything.

The next day, my daughter said to me, "You know better, Mom." I told her, "They shouldn't have tried to take me for a fool."

I was tired. I just wanted to be done with Jake and all his drama.

After a while, we moved back to Harlowe. One day, I saw her car again and noticed him down at the club. She was picking him up. By the time I got there, they were gone. That was the final straw.

That day, I packed his things and put him out for good. I was done. They could have each other.

I was a mother just trying to make it, and Jake was adding more stress to my life than anything else.

After leaving Jake's sister's house and washing my hands of him, things became a little calmer, at least for a while. Jake ended up moving to Atlantic City, which was near Morehead City. Around this time, I had a few fines I needed to pay off, and I ended up serving 30 days in jail. When I got out, I had no choice but to stay with Jake, bringing my baby and my son with me.

While living there, I ended up selling crack to him and his friends because I had no other income coming in. That was such a scary and desperate time for me. One day, Jake started acting out, so I called the cops, and they took him to jail. While he was locked up, I contacted my old landlord and was able to move into a place in New Bern, NC.

Once I moved, I started working two jobs and didn't have to sell drugs anymore, thank God. At that time, I was smoking weed and sometimes went to work high. I was just trying to cope with everything. During this time, I met a guy named Mustafa, but he turned out to be bad news. He was a liar, and strange things started happening when I was around him. For example, when I smoked weed with him, I noticed my high would last way longer than usual, which made me uneasy.

Weird things also started happening in my apartment. Sometimes the electricity would randomly shut off for no reason. I began to feel like I wasn't crazy, something was off.

One day, I was staying with a friend closer to town, and Mustafa and I went to a hotel to drop off some money I owed her. While we were there, Mustafa stole some toys from in front of the hotel. When we got in the car, he said, "They're for your baby." I was furious and asked him, "Why would you do that?"

Later that day, when I got back to my friend's house, she told me the police had been there looking for me. They left a note, so I immediately took the toys back to the hotel and explained the situation. They seemed like they wanted to arrest me, but I told them, "It wasn't me, I'm just returning the toys."

My blood pressure was through the roof because I thought I might go to jail for something I didn't even do. Thankfully, the police eventually caught Mustafa, and when I went to see him in jail, he had the audacity to ask if I was going to bail him out. I told him, "You made me lose my job, and you don't even care." That was it for me, I was done with him.

I truly believe Mustafa had bad intentions for me and my baby, so I became extra cautious. I stopped smoking weed completely because I knew I had to stay alert at all times.

In 2005, my sister and her husband came to visit me at my apartment. By this time, I had moved into a much nicer place. She told me about a job opening on the military base where she lived in Pennsylvania. My sister had gotten remarried and relocated there, so she encouraged me to apply. At first, I was hesitant because I was tired of moving. But eventually, I called her, and she submitted an application for me with the Department of Defense.

In April 2006, I was offered training for the job, which would last two weeks. I saved up for our bus tickets, and a friend helped me with the money for the third ticket I needed. We left for Pennsylvania, and I was both scared and excited about this new chapter.

Originally, my training was supposed to start in June 2006, but it got pushed to September. In the meantime, my children and I stayed with my oldest sister. While we had everything we needed, living with her was a challenge. She drank heavily, and when she was drunk, she would turn angry and start cussing and fussing. Thankfully, I didn't have to rely on her for much, but I could tell she was tired of us being there, even though she knew I was waiting for my training to start.

By July, I had transferred my CNA license to Pennsylvania and started working through temp agencies to save money. My sister let me use an extra car she had, as long as I paid the insurance. But one night, while I was at work, she called me to argue about the insurance. I told her, "How was I supposed to know it was due if you didn't tell me?" It became clear to me that some people would rather see you struggle than succeed.

She ended up taking the car back, so I learned the public transportation system quickly. I started working at a nursing home in Camp Hill, PA, and even worked doubles some days to save up for a place of my own.

During this time, I also noticed my baby sister started acting strangely toward me. To keep myself calm and avoid conflict, I prayed constantly. I was working overtime, determined to find a place for my children and me.

One day, I remembered a man I had met through one of the temp agencies and decided to call him. He ended up driving me around to look for a room to rent. Eventually, he offered to rent me a room at his own place. Since I had both of my children with me, I was cautious, but he never tried anything inappropriate. In fact, we ended up going to the same church, which I discovered when I saw him there one Sunday.

A kind, elderly man from church also helped by giving me rides to work and church. Everything was slowly coming together.

After my training ended, I had three homes to choose from. I chose the place that was closest to my job, just down the street. What a blessing!

In September 2006, I started working on the New Cumberland base, earning $20 an hour. I quit the nursing home job and began working full-time at the base. I prayed daily, asking God to guide me and help me keep this job for as long as possible. For the first time, I felt like I was truly moving forward in life.

Chapter 4

New Beginnings with new love

I lived in New Cumberland, and I walked to work because we were staying near the base at that time. I sent my oldest daughter and my grandson their bus tickets because I had to leave them in North Carolina until I was able to come up with enough money to bring them to me. They eventually caught the bus, and my daughter was pregnant with my second grandson. I was so happy that we were finally away from that place—a place full of depression.

Despite everything, I wasn't too worried about my son. He was always getting himself into trouble, but I felt a sense of relief knowing where he was when he was locked up. In 2006, we came down and he got into trouble in August of that year, which led to him being sent to a juvenile detention facility. I stayed focused on my plans and kept moving forward.

Not long after that, I met Chris. At the time, I was just trying to stay focused on my life, but he kindly introduced himself. After a while, I left New Cumberland and moved into a house in Harrisburg. Chris was really nice, and he treated my daughter Shantelle and my other children well. We dated for two years, and eventually, he asked me to marry him.

At that point, I was still married, but I began divorce proceedings. It was surprisingly easy because Jake, my then-husband, was in jail. Chris and I didn't have a big wedding. We got married at the Justice of the Peace office on July 31, 2007. We didn't have a honeymoon, but we were planning one, and that was okay with me.

Less than a year later, my son Demetius, who was 16 at the time, was on probation. He had a habit of being the "fall guy" for others.

One day, I told him to be home by midnight, but at 1:00 AM, he still wasn't home. Shortly after, I got a phone call from one of his friend's little brothers, telling me that Demetius and his friend had been shot.

When I got to the hospital, the doctors told me he had been shot four times, with one bullet missing the main artery near his heart by just an inch. I'm a praying mother, and I had always prayed for my children, asking God to guide them and protect them.

One of the doctors, whose name was Dr. Red Cross (a name I'll never forget), explained that they had to operate on Demetius. During the surgery, he died on the operating table three times, but they managed to save him. After the operation, he was in the hospital for a while. When he came home, it was a long process of recovery. However, it felt like he didn't fully take the situation seriously.

I continued to pray, asking God for guidance. Demetius couldn't keep food down, so I had to take him back to the doctor. They ended up inserting a balloon in his stomach to help him retain food. They also had to remove an inch of his large intestine because one of the bullets had damaged it. About six months later, I had to take him back to the hospital again because one of the bullets was pressing against his rib and trying to come out. The doctors removed it.

Meanwhile, Chris was dealing with his own struggles. He had been in a car accident before I met him and had titanium in his hip, which caused him constant pain. I later realized that he was taking more than just pain pills to cope with it, though he didn't know that I knew.

Fast forward to August 2, 2008. Chris started behaving strangely. He didn't come home for a couple of days and said he couldn't find his phone. A few days before this, I noticed that every time he used the restroom, it smelled like rotten eggs. I told him he needed to see a doctor, but he didn't take it seriously.

On August 4, 2008, I discovered that he had been taking money out of our joint account without telling me. I immediately closed the account. I worked from home on my computer in the back of the house, and I remember praying, "God, I didn't ask for this."

On August 10, 2008, at midnight, Chris came home. I was lying on my left side in bed. He had a habit of pretending something was wrong whenever he had done something wrong. This time, he said, "I have a pain in my chest." I didn't believe him at first, but then all of a sudden, I felt cold water on the bed. He had dropped a cup of water, and it spilled everywhere.

So, I got up, and I felt him, and called 911. As I was getting Shantelle ready to go to the hospital, I went downstairs and realized he was gone. I called a cab, and after what felt like an hour, it finally arrived. We made it to the hospital, and they took us back to where he was. He was still experiencing v-tach (ventricular tachycardia).

Chris told me he was sorry for everything he had ever done, and shortly after that, he had his final attack. The doctors worked on him, but every time they stopped doing chest compressions, he flatlined again. They eventually took us out of the room and sat us in a waiting area. Around 6 a.m., they came to tell us that he had passed away.

I didn't know how to feel. I cried and started making phone calls. I called his sisters, my sister, and my daughter to tell them the news. They came to the hospital to support me. I had never experienced anything like that before.

At 7 a.m., my sister and brother-in-law took us to their house. I stayed there for one night and then returned home. One of Chris's sisters offered to handle the obituary, but she didn't include certain people, which caused some issues. It was a mess, but I dealt with it.

I went to pick out his casket and clothes for the funeral. He was laid to rest on August 13, and we took a photo together at his gravesite. His funeral was so packed with people. Our life together wasn't bad, but Chris had hidden secrets that he didn't want to share. If he had just opened up and told me what he was dealing with, we could have prayed about the situation and left it in God's hands. But it's neither here nor there now.

After the funeral, I went back home. At the time, we were in the process of buying the house we lived in. When Chris passed, the landlord, John, created a new lease that I had to sign. It felt as though he was starting everything over, as if we had just begun the process again. But anyway, John agreed to cover anything over $500 that needed to be fixed in the house, which was fair.

Chris had made sure we were taken care of financially, and I decided to start renovating the house. I hired a guy who was a friend of one of my friends, but I later realized he was taking advantage of me. Unfortunately, I didn't figure it out until halfway through the project. I managed to get the house renovated from upstairs to downstairs with new carpet and everything.

Even though I had moments of mixed emotions, I got through it. Slowly, things started to feel somewhat normal again. I returned to work after missing 30 days, but I began to truly realize the depth of my grief. I had never dealt with anything like this before, and no one could tell me how to process it—I had to figure it out on my own.

My neighbors would check on me, and for the most part, I was doing okay.

Chapter 5

What does love have to do with it!

I think a lot of times, as adults, we believe we know what we're doing, but in reality, it often backfires when it's not aligned with God's plan. That's when we end up in a mess.

In 2007, I met Joshua, and we became friends. He was cool. By 2008, after my husband Chris passed away, there were several men who liked me, but Joshua stood out to me. He was in the military, and I thought maybe he would be a little different. I believed he could help bring stability and not cause unnecessary problems or drama. I've always liked the whole military vibe, so I thought, Why not?

I was comfortable with him. I guess you could call it the beginning of a disaster, though! Anyway, he asked me out, and I said yes. He wanted to take me to church, which was something I really appreciated. One night, we were talking on the phone, and he ended up coming over. After that night, he never left.

Looking back, what I put up with then, I would never tolerate now. Don't get me wrong—he paid bills and tried to act accordingly, but you can only fake it for so long. I'm not saying I don't make mistakes, but at least I'm open to someone kindly pointing them out. If you're rude about it, I automatically shut down.

At the time, Chris had bought me a burgundy Grand Prix, and I had bought an SUV afterward. Joshua, on the other hand, had an old beat-up truck that sometimes wouldn't even start. So, I ended up letting him use the SUV since I drove the car most of the time, and that wasn't a problem for me.

However, Joshua had a gambling problem. He liked playing numbers and scratch-offs, and he would try to get me to do it too. I always told him how I felt about gambling and how I didn't believe the whole thing about the money going to support senior citizens or anything like that.

Joshua also had some child support issues involving a son that wasn't actually his. It was one of those situations where they claimed the child was his, and he just went along with it. Joshua would ask me several times, "Do you think the child even looks like me?" And I'd say, "No! Why don't you go get a DNA test?"

Eventually, he did, and it turned out the boy wasn't his. But by then, Joshua had already been paying child support for years—the child was 18 years old at that point. After this, I noticed a change in his attitude and manners.

He started going to church, but I realized he was only going for me, not for himself. That lasted about two years. After that, he became distant, and the communication between us started to fade. We still talked a little, but it wasn't the same.

We had been planning to get married, and let me tell you, the whole process of "loving the unlovable" felt very real, y'all. So many times before the wedding, I told him to leave, or he'd say, "We don't have to get married." Honestly, I was praying that he meant it!

When it came to the wedding planning, I tried my best to keep things on track. We worked with someone to do the decorations. I'm not much of a talkative person, but I did try to communicate with people at first. After a while, though, I shut them out, and Joshua began handling most of the calls. It was a lot to deal with.

I did set up the wedding colors, chose my bridesmaids and maid of honor, and picked out the shoes and other things we needed. When it came time for Joshua and his groomsmen, as well as his best man, to get their suits, I directed him on what to do. It was perfect.

Image was everything to him, and I often found myself trying to impress him with my clothes. I had a lot of outfits, and I considered them nice. During that time, I wore heels frequently and dressed up even just to go to the store. He liked my legs, so I sometimes wore shorter dresses or skirts. All in all, I was trying to satisfy him.

I tried to share my past with him so he could understand the different triggers I had. I also encouraged him to do the same, but he thought it wasn't important, so I let it go for a while. We worked side by side at the Department of Defense, on the same shift, and even small things would upset him. Talk about being mad at life—my God! What was I doing?

There were times I could joke with him, but one day that changed. He snapped—wow. As the wedding approached, his best friend came down, and they all went out. Then it was time. Everyone arrived, but the wedding started a little late. I still remember walking down the aisle with my stomach flipping. I should have turned around right then, but after all the hard work, time, and effort everyone put into it, I kept going. My brother-in-law walked me down the aisle, and when I got to Joshua, he smelled like alcohol. I was just like, "Ugh!"

The wedding was over, and then it was time for the reception. Everything was nice. We ate, danced, and took pictures. My brother came all the way from Delaware, which was so thoughtful, and my sisters were there too. Two of my sisters were in the wedding, along with my daughter and one of his girls as bridesmaids.

The very next morning, we headed to Myrtle Beach for our honeymoon and stayed for seven days. It was a great time. We enjoyed the rooftop views, a cruise boat with slot machines and dinner—it was all so fun for me. We also went horseback riding on the beach at sunrise, and it was absolutely beautiful!

So, we headed home after extending our honeymoon by one extra day. During the trip, we ended up getting a timeshare, which allowed us to get deals on vacations and travel anywhere. Once we returned home, life with Joshua began. For a while, things were fine—we talked, laughed, and joked around. But over time, things began to shift. I could no longer joke with him or even laugh without feeling like I was walking on eggshells. That familiar, numbing feeling returned, and I hated it.

Joshua was becoming my nightmare. There was no life in his eyes, but I thought love could override that. Boy, was I wrong. Every day started to feel like I was riding with a stranger. We used to say the Our Father prayer together, but even that stopped. I found myself praying alone.

By this time, I had been at the Department of Defense (DOD) for about five years, but things weren't good—neither at home nor at work. I ended up hurting my shoulder, and they placed me on light duty in another department. That separation from Joshua was peaceful because I didn't have to see him during lunch or breaks. I only saw him when we went home, and even that felt like too much. People assumed everything was fine between us, but I'm a very private person. I don't share my marriage problems with anyone unless I absolutely need to—or unless I've reached a point where I no longer care about the other person's feelings.

In April 2012, I left the DOD to focus on myself. During this time, I began feeding the homeless and even thought about opening a shelter. However, that plan fell through, which turned out to be a blessing because I realized I wasn't fully trained for such a big undertaking. Instead, I went back to my work as a CNA, which made me happy. Joshua wasn't thrilled about it, but I also started going to GED classes because I was determined to get my diploma.

It took me two attempts, but I finally earned my GED. This accomplishment was deeply personal because it was something from my past that I had tried to share with Joshua, but he never wanted to listen. If he had listened, maybe things could have turned out differently. I was in my 40s, going back to school, and I was so proud of myself. I had always told my children not to give up on their education, to at least get a diploma. Both my daughter and my son eventually earned their GEDs, and that was such a relief for me. I've always believed that knowledge is something no one can take away from you.

When it came time for my GED graduation, I showed Joshua the invitation. He seemed shocked—I don't know why. I told him, "You saw what you wanted to see and didn't want to talk about anything, so don't act surprised now." He didn't come to my graduation, but my children did, and that was all the support I needed. Afterward, I had already signed up for an RN program. By the time my classes started, I was ready.

I began my journey with so much determination that nothing could stop me. However, when I started my chemistry classes, I was having severe issues with Joshua. The stress became too much, and I couldn't finish the RN program. I didn't want to give up on school entirely, so I decided to enroll in a Medical Assistant program instead. I started attending Brightwood Career Institute in May 2016, and I graduated in December of the same year.

This time, Joshua did come to my graduation, along with my pastors and my daughter.

Oh, and I forgot to tell you about the cruise trip we took to the Bahamas! It was a good trip overall. As we boarded the ship, we went through the whole process of getting our cruise cards. The staff explained that only one card could be used for purchases on the ship. Joshua wasn't happy about this, but I was laughing on the inside because he hated buying anything for me. This was his payback.

The cruise was excellent, but we didn't have much to talk about, and he was mad about that. Well, y'all, everything I said never seemed to make sense to him because I didn't see things the way he did. When we returned home, it felt like we had never left. This time, though, he brought back gifts for his friends—bottles of White Hennessy. That made me stop and think. Buying alcohol for his friends wasn't a problem for him, but putting gas in my car when I needed it was? I couldn't see the logic in that.

Our total time together ended up being 10 years. Throughout our marriage, he was very verbally and emotionally abusive. Now, I'm not saying I'm an angel, but I've always made it a point not to bring drama into the home. In the last year or so of our relationship, I started sleeping on the recliner with my Bible, the remote, and my gospel music. That space gave me peace. I also began walking in the mornings at 7 a.m., using that time to talk to God and worship. It was good for me.

In June 2016, we were having a family reunion in Delaware. I asked Joshua if he wanted to go, but he said no. Still, I felt it was the right thing for me to do. So, it was me, my oldest and youngest daughters, and my three grandchildren who made the trip. We started early that morning, around 7 a.m. Before we got to Delaware, my two daughters switched seats—my youngest moved to the front, and my oldest sat in the back.

As we got closer, I started feeling uneasy. In fact, that strange feeling in my stomach had been there before that day. I prayed and prayed as we drove. When we got to Dover, Delaware, we were approaching a traffic light. Suddenly, the Holy Spirit told me to place my hands firmly on the steering wheel and not to look back. Of course, I glanced at my rearview mirror, but I didn't turn around. I knew that if I did, my children might have looked too—and Lord only knows what could have happened.

It was like a demonic figure was coming up behind me. I braced myself, and then he crashed right into my car. The impact totaled the vehicle, and I was a mess. My oldest daughter was knocked out for a few seconds. My youngest daughter was okay, and my grandchildren were mostly fine. My oldest grandson had a scratch on the side of his face, my little grandson's wrist was broken, and my granddaughter was just scared but unharmed.

When I came back to my senses after the crash, I saw traffic coming from both directions. All I could do was say, "Thank you, Lord," but I was terrified—terrified for my children and grandchildren. A lady came up behind me and asked, "Who hit you?" I replied, "Who hit us?" When I turned around, the car that hit us was gone.

 The police were called, and they came. They found the car down the highway, flipped over the median where he had tried to get away (God is good in every way). The police began asking questions and everything, and they asked if I had someone to call. So, we called Joshua and told him what had happened, but he was so nonchalant about the whole thing, as if it wasn't serious.

Anyway, we were taken to the hospital and checked over. My back was bothering me a little, but my crew was okay, except for my grandson, who ended up with his wrist in a cast. At this point, I was totally embarrassed because the man I was married to wasn't even trying to come and get us.

To lighten the mood, my grandson made a joke and said, "Why don't we go to a hotel?" So, I said, "Yes, why not?" and we went. I called my sister to let her know what was going on, but she said something strange. She asked, "Are you still coming to the family reunion?" Later that night, my cousin and her children came by, and I was thankful for their visit.

The very next day, my son-in-law came to get us, and I prayed the whole way back to Harrisburg, PA, that Joshua wouldn't be there. I was just speechless about how he had been acting. When I got home, he wasn't there, and I was relieved because I didn't even know what to say to him. Later on, he came in, but he never asked any questions or showed any concern.

The following Sunday, we went to his church. After the service, I saw my girlfriend, and my spirit told me to ask her if she knew about the accident. The way she was talking made me curious, so I said, "Did you know I was in an accident?" She said, "No!" I told her what had happened, and she simply said, "I'm glad you're okay."

When we got home, I went to the bedroom after we'd changed and stood at the door. He was lying down, and I asked him, "Did you tell anyone or even get some prayer for us?" He got mad, as usual, and said, "I do things the way I do them, and you do what you want to do." I just shook my head, giggled, and said, "Okay," then walked away and went back to the living room.

At this point, it was time for me to start physical therapy. I was also in school, working on my medical assistant license. I attended a school called Kaplan, which is now known as Brightwood Career Institute in Harrisburg, PA. Most of the time, I had to call a cab to get to therapy. But I'll tell you, God is good.

During my first week back to school and therapy, there was a young man in my class who drove a cab. Not only did he start picking me up for school, but he also came in the mornings to take me to therapy.

Now it was time to do some thinking. I was in a predicament, but I'm so glad I believed in God. I had seen so many things that were definitely out of whack during this time. While I was going to therapy and looking for another vehicle, Joshua was so mean and negative about everything I said.

At one point, I was offered a vehicle. A young lady took me to look at it, and I was there for hours. To make this story short, all the paperwork was in order. However, at the very end, while I was talking to the sales manager, he began sharing his own struggles with his failed marriage. Then, all of a sudden, there was a mess-up with the paperwork, and I couldn't get the car. I wasn't upset because I kept saying, "God has a plan!"

When I finally knew I was going to get another vehicle, I told Joshua that I might need some insurance. He turned around and said, "We can't be on the same insurance anymore." All I could think about was how, before my accident, he had been on my insurance. Then I found out that, during the time between my accident, therapy, and looking for another vehicle, he had let the insurance lapse instead of properly canceling it.

The very next Monday, the salesman called me from Lebanon Hyundai, the same place I had been to earlier. He said, "I have a vehicle that just came in. Would you like to look at it?" I said, "Yes, could you please send me pictures of it?" He did, and it was a 2011 black Toyota Camry. At that point, I just needed a vehicle, so I went in, did the paperwork, and got the car.

By the way, I was juggling two full-time jobs, a part-time job, and school back then. I was working on my MA license, but I was going through a lot, so I decided to take a step back from school for a while.

When I got home, he was at work, and I couldn't wait to show him the car the next day. When I finally did, he wasn't happy about anything. He saw the car and said, "You're still doing things by yourself." I asked him what he could have done differently, but I already knew. He had done everything but physically beat me down. The verbal abuse sometimes hurt worse than physical abuse ever could.

I kept thinking about the times he had left me stranded. I remembered one time he left me in Delaware and another time when I was at my job. He was supposed to pick me up, and I called him three times. Each time, he said he was on his way, but he never showed up. Finally, I told him, "Don't worry about it. I'll just call a cab." I was so tired. The very next night, I had to work again, so that's exactly what I did.

That morning, after my shift ended, I went to my part-time job at the research office. That day, my supervisor was getting on my last nerve, and it was all over a camera I had forgotten to return over the weekend. I had apologized, but she kept going on and on about it. I didn't know what else she wanted me to say. I finally left, told her, "Have a blessed day," and I never went back to that office again.

After that, I applied for a job at a place called Spring Pine in Harrisburg. I started working there, but after a while, I became very uncomfortable. I saw so many things that disturbed me. Often, I would go inside one of the rooms, cry, and pray.

About 7 or 8 months into working there, it was a cold winter day, and my car's battery died. To make a long story short, I wasn't able to move the car, so I left it in the parking lot. I told Joshua about it, but he did nothing. I just wanted to see what he would do, but I wasn't surprised when he didn't offer to help.

A week later, when I got paid, I bought a battery. The sales manager asked me, "Are you the one who called about a battery and said you needed someone to install it?" I said, "Yes." He responded, "I'll bring it myself and attach it for you—no charge." All I could say was, "Thank you, Jesus!" My God was working.

Even during this time, I wasn't happy. By then, I had been married for at least seven years, and while it wasn't all bad, 75% of my marriage was a mess. There was no communication, no emotional connection, and I always felt like I couldn't say anything without him insulting me.

Between 2016 and 2017, I left Joshua for the first time. I was sick and tired of his behavior and his constant insults about everything.

I remember him coming to my new church home. He just wanted to come in, look around, and find something negative to say because he was so miserable. Shantelle and I were living in an apartment complex, and she wanted to try public school again. I decided to let her. She had a difficult time adjusting at first, but eventually, we worked on her studies together. Homeschool and public school had very different curriculums.

She joined musicals, and she always excelled in dance or anything else that caught her interest. I loved watching her dance and seeing her develop other passions besides boys. She was involved in jazz, hip hop, ballet, and gymnastics. She had dance classes three times a week, and once a year, we would attend a dance competition called Monsters. Not once did my husband ever come to the competition or contribute financially to her dance expenses.

I've always been a hard worker, but during those times, I had to work even harder. Most of the time, her dance teacher would cover the costs for some students, and we would pay her back. I thought this was such a blessing. I was happy for Shantelle and the direction her life was heading.

Then, after a while, I let the devil back into my life. He started coming over to my apartment, and I fell behind on some bills. Fear began to take over me, so I told him I was coming back. He acted like he was happy, but he really wasn't—because now he had to see me all the time. I thought things were okay because we had been spending time together. We even went to Vegas for a business trip, but that didn't last. A lot of craziness kept happening.

During this time, his dad was sick, and his mom had Alzheimer's, which was getting worse. One night, he got a phone call saying she was on the rooftop with a can of house spray, claiming someone was trying to break in. Months later, she had to stay between our house and his son's house. For some reason, he would get mad at me when she would go outside and walk down the road.

I told him, "I work two jobs and go to school. You expect me to stay up all day and watch her while she runs up and down the sidewalk—even at night while you're home?" She would sneak out the door and leave it open. After a while, they put her in a nursing home, where she eventually passed away.

One year, his friend was getting married, and he wanted us to dress alike for the wedding. I was excited, so he ordered a dress for me and everything. But as time passed, he started treating me so badly that I couldn't fake it anymore—even in public. I wanted to see if he would follow through with his promises. As the wedding day grew closer, he never said anything else about it. When the day came, he got dressed and left. Not only did he attend one wedding—he went to two.

I was completely drained, emotionally and physically. I began to separate myself. I started sleeping in the living room, which became my space of peace. I found comfort in my Bible and gospel music. I would wake up early to walk, talk to God, and cry. Then, I'd pull myself together and get Shantelle ready for school.

I had a lot of decisions to make. Both my daughter and I needed peace. I finally made up my mind—I was going to leave. Around this time, I had injured my foot and was starting a new journey. I landed my first client for my home health business. Surprisingly, even in all this, he never knew I had started my own business.

The best decision I ever made was to step out on faith, knowing that God was holding my hand every step of the way. One day in 2012, I ran into an old church member. I didn't know much about her, but she seemed nice enough. She had just come back from Virginia and didn't have anywhere to live, so I offered her a room in my home until she could find a place of her own. I let her move in, even though my husband wasn't too thrilled about it.

After a while, she told me she was pregnant. Being the person I am, I was so excited for her. I even offered to take her to her doctor appointments, but she always said no. I didn't think much of it at the time. As time went on, I would check in with her and ask if the baby was okay. She would always say yes, so I left it at that.

As the weather warmed up, some strange things started happening. One night, my husband, Shantelle, and I went out, and when we came back home, we found she had brought a guy into the house. I walked in and asked, "What are you doing? This is not your house." I told her that Joshua was going to say something, and sure enough, he came in and asked, "Who is this? This is not your house." He told the guy to leave and then told her, "You don't pay any bills here, so don't bring anyone into this house again." That was the end of that situation, but it left me uneasy.

By summer, I had started thinking about opening a shelter. I told her about my idea, and she just so happened to find a place that would be perfect for it. I got in contact with the property owners, and they gave me a monthly price. I decided to move forward, so I rented the house and got the utilities hooked up. I ordered desks and other items we would need for the shelter.

I had already started feeding the homeless with the help of about five people, including my daughter. Most of the time, I would cook at home and take the food to them. I loved doing things like this, but one Sunday, we went to deliver food, and they told us that people were no longer allowed to bring meals to that location.

After that, we focused on fixing up the shelter. We started spreading the word, and I began accepting people into the house. I decided to let the pregnant woman manage the shelter. Despite this, I couldn't shake the feeling that something wasn't right. For months, I worked hard to fix up the place. We would pray some nights and talk to the clients. Each client had their own room.

There was one lady, Ms. Terry, who was a reader and kept to herself. I never had any problems with her. However, the rest of the people, including the manager, began giving me a headache. I threw the manager a baby shower, and we all went to eat at Country Buffet.

A few months went by. During that time, the state came to inspect the property. They gave me some time to make repairs. I later found out that the copper pipes in the house had been stolen and sold for money. I warned everyone about what was going on and what might happen, but some people just don't believe anything until they're knee-deep in trouble.

I was up to my head with them, and my patience was running thin. I didn't blame anyone but myself for the situation. My daughter

Tekeyia told me, "Mom, something is not right about that pregnancy." She explained that the woman's husband used to go to her husband's barber shop to get his hair cut and had warned them about her. Believe it or not, my husband at the time had told me the same thing.

Months went by, and she was still supposedly pregnant. Then one day, she called me while I was out taking care of some business. I decided to stop by the hospital to check on her. My spirit didn't pick up on anything strange, so I went. There were people at the hospital, but no one said anything about the baby. Even the pastor and her daughter came and prayed for her.

I left and returned to the shelter to take care of some things, but the Holy Spirit kept urging me to call the hospital. The first time, I ignored it. The second time, I ignored it again. By the third time, I finally called—it was around 7:45 p.m. I spoke with the nurse who was taking care of her. Something felt off because she wasn't on the maternity floor.

I asked the nurse how she was doing, and then I asked, "How long do they keep the babies in the morgue?" The nurse responded, "I don't know, but what does that have to do with her?" I explained, "She told me she had a miscarriage." The nurse replied, "No, she wasn't here for that."

Now, the timing of this conversation was critical because the nurse's shift ended at 7 p.m. She didn't know that I had called or that I now knew the truth—this woman was never pregnant. For the next three days, I played along as if I believed her, but eventually, I couldn't take it anymore.

I confronted her and said, "Please stop lying. Just stop." She insisted, "I was pregnant." I told her, "No, you weren't." She asked, "How do you know?" So, I explained that I had spoken with the nurse. She became furious. Had I not called the hospital, I never would have known the truth.

A couple of weeks went by, and I was praying and talking to God about how to place the shelter residents somewhere else. But God stepped in, and I didn't have to do anything. The guy from the state called and said he was coming to shut the place down because the residents were engaging in inappropriate activities in the house. I told him, "I'll meet you there."

I decided to take the residents to the farthest motel I could find. I paid for one night and didn't answer their calls or anything after that. Later, I found out that they had stolen a woman's car—one of the ladies staying at the shelter—and taken it to Virginia.

One day, I came home and found Ms. Terry, the quiet woman who used to stay at the shelter, sitting on my doorstep. She told me she had nowhere to go. My heart was weak, and I couldn't turn her away, so I let her sleep in the basement.

Now, Joshua never went into the basement, but that particular night—or early morning—he did. Who did he see? Ms. Terry. All I could say was, "I'll make sure she's gone later on." The next morning, I dropped her off at the hospital because she was suicidal, and I didn't know how to handle that. They kept her for 72 hours, and I never saw her again.

Taylor, the woman who lied about being pregnant, tried to reach out to me a few months later, but I didn't respond.

This entire experience taught me a powerful lesson. My heart is always open to helping others, but I learned that you must use wisdom in all situations. The Bible tells you that the issues of life flows from the heart. And it's always true.

Chapter 6

Escaping a Narcissist and being able to tell the story!

Living with a narcissist is a traumatic experience. It plays a big part in your mental health. A lot . people, regardless of gender, can become depressed as a result of this. We experience anxiety, sit with depression, and feel emotionally drained. When living with a narcissist, you are always blamed for everything. Anything that goes wrong is your fault in their eyes. They are never wrong, and if you even try to say otherwise, they will argue with you relentlessly. To cope, you build walls and become extremely careful about how you express yourself. Often, you stop talking altogether. Even the people closest to you may not know you are suffering because you try to protect the person you are with.

In 2008, studies showed that 7.7% of men and 4.8% of women suffered from narcissistic personality disorder. Many people stay in relationships with narcissists for various reasons: trying to make the relationship work, financial dependence, or even moments of hope that things might improve. However, when you return home after feeling hopeful, you find yourself invisible again. Narcissists are content as long as you play their game and stay within their boundaries. But the moment you begin to express your feelings or stand up for yourself, they turn on you. At that point, you are treated like an outsider.

The truth is, you cannot change these people. As much as you pray for their hearts to change, it won't happen unless they genuinely want it. My faith has taught me that if a person does not want to change their heart, they won't. Narcissistic behavior has been increasing, and it doesn't discriminate by age—it can affect anyone.

This disorder often comes with an addictive need for validation. Social media can amplify these tendencies, further fueling the disorder.

My real-life experience left me mentally, emotionally, and verbally abused. I was with my narcissist for 10 years—9 of those years living with him. By the grace of God, I managed to escape from this toxic relationship. My strength came from Him. I began my own form of therapy by separating myself from him, even while we were still in the same house. I moved into the living room and started sleeping on the recliner. During that time, I poured myself into my business, listened to worship music, and kept my Bible close. That period of separation gave me pure peace.

But it wasn't just me who was affected; my daughter was, too. For a long time, I didn't fully understand what was happening. Then one day, I happened to listen to a show discussing narcissistic personality disorder. That was my turning point. I began researching and reading about it, and everything finally made sense. It was a true eye-opener.

God ultimately pulled me from the grip of this narcissist, but by the time it was over, I was completely drained. I struggled to make sense of everything. Over time, I found my voice again, rebuilt my self-esteem, and realized that I survived because God protected me. I held onto my composure and integrity throughout it all. My church became my refuge, and one of my clients played a significant role in my healing journey.

It has been six years since I escaped, and while I have lost some things, I have regained my happiness and peace. Narcissistic behavior is often dismissed as mere arrogance, but it can deeply affect the lives of those around them. If a person isn't strong enough, they can lose their mind, sink into depression, and struggle to recover. You begin to feel guilty for things that aren't your fault.

You lose yourself trying to satisfy someone who will never be satisfied.

Thankfully, some people snap out of this time warp and realize they need to leave. They must find the courage to get out. Narcissists often make you feel like you can't survive without them. You question how you'll make it on your own. But when you take a step back, you realize you've always been capable. With planning, prayer, and determination, you can execute your plan of escape and reclaim your life.

To my readers, I thank you for throwing a seed my way. In this short book, there are lessons to be learned about life. There is certainly a process in understanding the order in which we choose to go through life. Some paths lead us down a downward spiral, while others allow us to experience something called faith—learning how to trust God in the midst of your storm and understanding that there is a waiting period for everything. My life was a little twisted from the beginning. As a young girl, I didn't understand my purpose in life. I found myself living in someone else's mess and in a life I couldn't make sense of. But as time went on, I came to know that there is a God I could pray to, a God who answers prayers. God is a God of love. He doesn't want you to think you have to be perfect to come to Him. He doesn't require much—only that you come to Him, seek to understand His ways, and love Him. He loves you because He created you in His image. He will never leave you nor forsake you. He loves you!

One thing I know for sure is that when you allow God into your heart, you are covered by His grace and mercy. I encourage you to study these scriptures and take them to heart. And if you want to be saved, know that it's never too late to open your heart to Him.

please contact me : godschildren22@yahoo. com

I. Proverbs 3: 5 and 6 Trust in the lord

2. Matthew 17; 20 ;21 Faith Hebrews 13 ;8 Grace and Mercy Hebrews 13;5;6 Never leave you

Romans 1 O; 9 Asking God to come into your heart

Made in the USA
Middletown, DE
09 February 2025